AF606711

DIERKS BENTLEY

Tammy Gagne

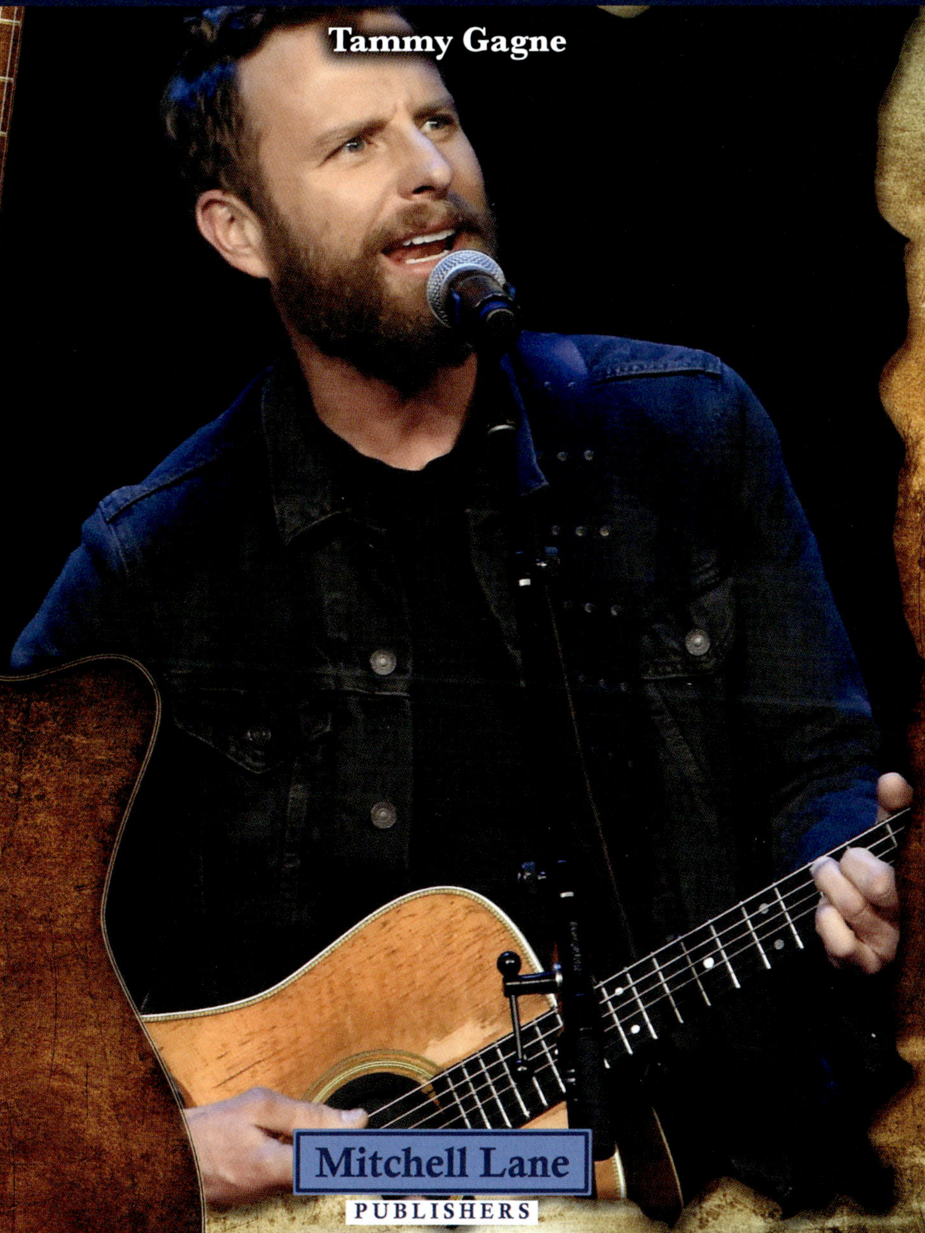

Mitchell Lane
PUBLISHERS
2001 SW 31st Avenue
Hallandale, FL 33009
www.mitchelllane.com

Printing 1 2 3 4 5 6 7 8 9

Brett Eldridge
Chris Stapleton
Dierks Bentley

Eric Church
Jake Owen
Kacey Musgraves

Designer: Sharon Beck
Editor: Jim Whiting

Library of Congress Cataloging-in-Publication Data
Names: Gagne, Tammy, author.
Title: Dierks Bentley / by Tammy Gagne.
Description: Hallandale, FL : Mitchell Lane Publishers, [2018] | Series: Country's newest stars | Includes bibliographical references and index.
Identifiers: LCCN 2017046719 | ISBN 9781680201567 (library bound)
Subjects: LCSH: Bentley, Dierks—Juvenile literature. | Country musicians—United States—Biography—Juvenile literature.
Classification: LCC ML3930.B442 G34 2018 | DDC 782.421642092 [B] —dc23
LC record available at https://lccn.loc.gov/2017046719

eBook ISBN: 9-781-6802-157-4

ABOUT THE AUTHOR: Tammy Gagne has written more than 200 books for both adults and children. Her recent titles include several books about country music artists, including *Eric Church* and *Jake Owen*. She resides in northern New England with her husband and son.

PUBLISHER'S NOTE: The following story has been thoroughly researched and to the best of our knowledge represents a true story. While every possible effort has been made to ensure accuracy, the publisher will not assume liability for damages caused by inaccuracies in the data and makes no warranty on the accuracy of the information contained herein. This story has not been authorized or endorsed by Dierks Bentley.

PHOTO CREDITS: Design elements: (vintage paper guitar lake scene)—RhaStudio/iStock/Getty Images Plus, (star)—Andre_/DigitalVision Vectors/Getty Images, (abstract grunge)—Chen Ping-hung/Hemera/Getty Images Plus, (Contents background)—bobvidler/DigitalVision Vectors, (back matter banner)— fatmayilmaz/DigitalVision Vectors; cover, pp. 1, 5, 8, 9, 15, 23, 24—Rick Diamond/Staff/Getty Images Entertainment; p. 7—Gustavo Caballero/Staff/Getty Images Entertainment; pp. 14, 27—Kevin Winter/Staff/Getty Images Entertainment; p. 17—Larry Busacca/Staff/Getty Images Entertainment; p. 21—Michael Loccisano/Staff/Getty Images Entertainment; p. 24—Ethan Miller/Staff/Getty Images Entertainment.

CONTENTS

1 Live and In Person

Carson had been practicing for his middle school talent show for weeks. Now his big moment was almost here. In just a few moments he would be performing his favorite country song on his guitar in front of all his friends, family, and teachers. He knew the words and chords by heart. He just hoped he wouldn't make a fool of himself.

As the curtain rose, Carson pictured Dierks Bentley on the stage at the Talking Stick Resort Arena in Phoenix, Arizona the previous August. It was the first live concert Carson had ever attended. It was a birthday gift from his mother, who took him. Most kids his age wanted cell phones or video games. But all Carson wanted was to see his idol play live. Dierks hadn't seemed nervous at all. He just walked onto the stage and started strumming. If Dierks could perform in front of thousands of fans night

Dierks hadn't seemed nervous at all. He just walked onto the stage and started strumming.

Performing live is one of Dierks Bentley's favorite parts of being a country music singer.

after night, Carson thought, he could do it once in the auditorium of his school.

For the next three minutes, Carson belted out the lyrics to Dierks's hit single "Free and Easy (Down the Road I Go)" just as he had when he practiced the song earlier that afternoon. As he steadied the whammy bar at the end of the song, the audience began clapping and cheering. Even his crabby math teacher, who never

Dierks has compared making albums to putting jet fuel into an airplane.

smiled, seemed to enjoy the performance. At that moment, Carson was sure he knew exactly how Dierks Bentley felt when he performed.

Perhaps the excitement the country superstar feels for his music is contagious. At one time, Dierks saw records as tickets to his own performances. They made his tours possible and successful. Dierks has compared making albums to putting jet fuel into an airplane. Everything is about the performance.

And Dierks hasn't lost a bit of that love for performing. He says that he enjoys performing on such a deep level that virtually nothing could tear him away from going on tour. "Being on stage, it's such a high," he told Alison Bonaguro of CMT News. "It's like running a marathon. You just can't get that feeling anywhere else." Marathoning seems to run in the family. His wife Cassidy ran the 2017 Boston Marathon to raise money for Safe Haven, a shelter for homeless families in Nashville, Tennessee.

Topping the Charts

After numerous hits as an independent artist, in 2016 Dierks released "Different for Girls," a duet with Elle King. The song reached the top spot on the Mediabase

Dierks and fellow artist Elle King performed their duet, "Different for Girls," at the 50th annual Country Music Association (ACM) Awards in 2016.

chart and Billboard Country Airplay chart in September. It became the 15th number-one song of Dierks's career. It was also named the Country Music Association's Vocal Event of the Year.

Because Dierks thought the song was heavier than what he normally records, he wanted to include a female voice. Although he didn't write the song himself, he is extremely proud of the way it turned out. He has said the opportunity was the kind that comes around once in a career.

Dierks thinks his musical style has grown up with him. "[I]f you want to continue to write your own songs, you've got to find deeper stuff to write about. You've got to go to different places. When I go onstage now and sing 'What Was I Thinkin'?,' I still feel like the same guy who wrote that song and I can feel that moment, but if I wrote it today [It was released in 2003], it probably wouldn't be as authentic. I'm not running through cornfields and the police isn't chasing me as much these days," he joked to *Billboard* magazine in 2016.

Dierks wasn't always the cool performer his fans see on stage today. But he knew early that he wanted to become one. When he was just six years old, he drew a picture of the rock star he dreamed of becoming. His teacher wrote "Nice story" on it. Dierks has joked that he would love to show her that picture now that he is a country music star. It is on display at the Country Music Hall of Fame and Museum.

Dierks gives an interview and performs at the Country Music Hall of Fame in 2016.

2
A Southwestern Boy

Frederick Dierks Bentley was born on November 20, 1975 in Phoenix, Arizona. He was the second child of Leon and Catherine Bentley. He grew up with an older sister, Vanessa, and a younger brother, Fife. The boys got their unusual names from their extended family. Both Dierks and Fife are last names on their mother's side. Leon and Catherine decided to use them as middle names instead.

Going by one's middle name is a family tradition for the Bentleys. Dierks has answered to his middle name for as long as he can remember. When he and his wife started their family, Dierks's mother actually became upset with him for not calling his kids by their middle names. Because it sounds so unusual, many people think that Dierks is a stage name. He explains that many people also say or spell it wrong.

Dierks has answered to his middle name for as long as he can remember.

Vanessa was a big music lover when the Bentley kids were growing up. Her passion for music rubbed off on Dierks. Although the family home included a piano, Dierks said no one ever played it. He used to joke that it was there to hold picture frames.

When Dierks was 14, he attended Lawrenceville School, a college prep school in New Jersey. During his time there, he discovered how much he enjoyed country music in particular. Whenever he heard it, it reminded him of home.

Hank Williams Jr.

He had been listening to other types of music and playing his guitar. As he explained to CMT, he was trying to figure out what he wanted to do with his life when a friend played him the Hank Williams, Jr. song "Man to Man." The song changed his life. As soon as he heard it, he knew what he wanted to do for a living. He stopped playing his electric guitar and bought an acoustic one instead.

After graduating from Lawrenceville School, Dierks enrolled at the University of Vermont. But he only stayed in New England for one year. As a sophomore, he transferred to Vanderbilt University in Nashville. Although he didn't finish college, the move to Nashville was the beginning of a different type of education for the future country star.

The Country Music Capital

Dierks still had a lot to learn about country music. Coming from Arizona, Dierks had a very different idea of country music from people living in Nashville. He grew up relating country music to the Western sounds of Waylon Jennings and Marty Robbins. He soon realized that country music included many other styles as well.

While visiting clubs in Nashville, Dierks realized how much he liked bluegrass music. He also discovered country music legends such as George Jones from the 1950s and 60s. Dierks calls Jones one of the greatest singers in history. In addition to Jones, his favorite singers include Frank Sinatra, Keith Whitley, and Merle Haggard. They all have a knack for singing about broken hearts. Dierks thinks it is an amazing thing to

George Jones

Dierks quickly learned that succeeding as a country singer would not be easy.

take that kind of experience and sing about it.

Dierks quickly learned that succeeding as a country singer would not be easy. No one seemed willing to give him a shot. Although the lack of interest was discouraging, he did not give up. When he couldn't pay his bills with music gigs, Dierks took a job at the Nashville Network, usually called TNN. It is a cable network with programming devoted to all aspects of country music. During the day he did research on classic country music. When he went home, he worked on his own music.

He made demos of his songs and sent them to people who worked in the music industry. Dierks says that he never really had a big break. He simply kept working at succeeding in the business. All that effort paid off when Capitol Records finally heard Dierks's music. The label signed him, and he released his first album in 2003. Called *Dierks Bentley*, the album included his first big hit, "What Was I Thinkin'?" The song helped the album go platinum. That means it sold more than one million copies.

Rising Up and Settling Down

Country music fans took to Dierks right away. "What Was I Thinkin'?" shot to the top spot on the Billboard Country chart. Although it only spent two weeks at number one, the catchy tune earned him a big award—Best New Artist—at the 2004 Academy of Country Music awards. Years later, he still treasures the memory of that evening.

He wore a white collared shirt. It stuck in his mind because he had been on the road a long time, and hadn't dressed up in a while. He had no idea what to expect at the event, since he was so new to the concept of awards shows. He just remembers hearing his name being called, along with the title of ACM New Artist of the Year. He loved being able to walk on stage to hold up the trophy and thank everyone who had helped him earn the honor.

He loved being able to walk on stage to hold up the trophy and thank everyone who had helped him earn the honor.

One of Dierks's most treasured memories from his career is winning the award for Best New Artist at the ACM Awards in 2004.

The success didn't go to Dierks's head, which is noticeably hatless. While many other country stars embrace cowboy hats, Dierks doesn't wear one. He has also noticed that none of his favorite country artists wear one either. Although he wore cowboy hats as a kid, Dierks doesn't feel that wearing one now would represent who he is.

As his music continued to rise up the charts and win more awards, Dierks kept working hard at writing and playing. He has said that country music is almost a religion for him. It inspires him to get up every morning and helps him deal with life's challenges.

Playing country music himself has also led Dierks to some great times.

Playing country music himself has also led Dierks to some great times. One evening he was playing a gig at Market Street Brewery in downtown Nashville when he spotted Vince Gill in the audience. Though Gill was there just to listen to some good music, Dierks invited him to perform along

Dierks is a big fan of country music legend Vince Gill, who is known for his own unique style.

with him. Having a jam session on stage with Gill was thrilling for Dierks. He deeply admires Gill's unique style. He plays his music his own way and, as Dierks has noticed, Gill also chooses not to wear a cowboy hat.

Sharing His Success

It seemed like the entire world was falling in love with Dierks Bentley. But at least one person had known for a long time just how special he is. Dierks met Cassidy Black when they were in the eighth grade. Although they dated when Dierks was 17, he wasn't ready for a serious relationship yet. Looking back, he now realizes that she was more mature than he was at the time. Still, he loved her smile and confidence.

They always kept in touch. He would see her when he came home during the summers. They also bumped into each other at weddings. They tried to keep their relationship going. But geography made it difficult. Cassidy lived in San Francisco, where she worked in advertising. With Dierks in Nashville, it was just too hard to make it work between them. Everything changed in 2005, though. Cassidy attended a concert Dierks performed in Las Vegas with George Strait. Dierks knew that the time was right. They were married at the end of year.

Dierks met Cassidy Black when they were in the eighth grade. Although they dated when Dierks was 17, he wasn't ready for a serious relationship yet.

Marriage seemed to agree with Dierks. Two weeks later, the singer nabbed his second top single, "Come a Little Closer." The love ballad was as about as different as it could be from his first number one. Dierks was showing his listeners that he had range. Although his success had not come quickly, he was also proving that he had staying power.

Dierks has said that he is especially grateful that much of his success has come since he and Cassidy were married. He went through many ups and downs in his early days. He was glad to have someone to go through those experiences—both good and bad—with him. He has said that his rise to fame has been a crazy ride. But at the same time he cannot deny how wonderful it has been.

Dierks and his wife Cassidy attend the 44th annual CMA Awards at the Bridgestone Arena in Nashville on November 10, 2010.

4 An Expanding Family and Musical Style

Dierks's career continued to thrive as he and Cassidy started their family in 2008. Their first daughter Evalyn, whom they call Evie, was born that year. Another daughter, Jordan, joined the family on Christmas Day in 2010. And in 2013, they welcomed a baby boy, Knox. Dierks says that his daughters actually helped prepare him for having a son. Like their father, the girls enjoy outdoor activities such as camping and fishing. Dierks plans to keep doing all those same things with his son as well as he gets older.

For years, Dierks's public image was quite different from the man he is at home. He had built a carefree reputation with songs early in his career like "Lots of Leavin' Left to Do" (2005) and "Free and Easy (Down the Road I Go)" the following year. To listen to this music, one would think that all he cared about was having a

For years, Dierks's public image was quite different from the man he is at home.

good time. "I was really carrying the torch for the single dude and my whole mantra was about being single," he told *Rolling Stone* in 2016. "It was like a train going full speed, [touring] 300 dates a year . . . . On some of my records in there, I was struggling to figure out who I was. The *Feel That Fire* record [which he released in 2009], I think, was where I reached the end of the road, where I needed to reboot."

By this time Dierks had racked up seven number 1 hits and six Grammy nominations. This success gave him the ability to branch out in his style. After singing about freedom so much, he finally felt he had the freedom to do something he truly wanted. His album *Up on the Ridge* (2010) was his first to feature only acoustic music. The title song was about leaving the city of Nashville for a rural setting. The lyrics were a metaphor for the trip Dierks was taking away from mainstream country music.

He took a big risk by recording *Up on the Ridge*. It wasn't like anything else he had ever released. It also wasn't like most of the albums that were topping the music charts at the time. While some people called the music bluegrass, it was actually a combination of bluegrass, honky tonk, and even a cover of a U2 song.

Dierks told *Billboard* magazine, "I knew I was walking away from an easier road, but that road wasn't taking me where I wanted to go. So I just made the decision to step away and make a record going back to my roots and how I started, kind getting off the grid and see what happens."

At the Controls

As Dierks was trying new things in his music career, he was also taking control of his busy schedule in a new way. Dierks had been interested in airplanes since his childhood. He spent three years taking flying lessons when he was trying to become a successful country artist. He started off in a 1971 Cessna 150, which he rented to accumulate flight time. Although it was an older plane, Dierks thought it was an ideal model for a beginning pilot. He says it was especially easy to land, something Dierks mastered quickly.

Today, Dierks has his pilot's license and flies his own Cirrus SR22T Xi. Having a private plane helps him spend more time with his family even when he is on tour.

Today, Dierks has his pilot's license and flies his own Cirrus SR22T Xi. Having a private plane helps him spend more time with his family, even when he is on tour. In addition to using it for recreational time with his wife and kids, he flies it back and forth to shows. Before he had the plane, he had to leave home the night before a concert. Now he can leave the morning of the same day as the show and have the previous day and night at with his family.

That extra time with them has become incredibly important to Dierks. He has learned that being a husband and father means making time whenever possible. Cassidy takes on many of the parenting responsibilities when he has to be away from home. But he doesn't want to miss out on the most important years of his kids' childhoods. He also misses them terribly when he's away from home.

Dierks attended the 2014 CMT Music awards in a pilot's uniform.

5 Down the Road He Goes

Now that Dierks is famous, he uses his celebrity status for good causes. One of them is his Miles and Music for Kids motorcycle ride and concert, which he founded in 2006. The annual event has raised a total of more than $3 million for a children's hospital in Nashville. In addition to lending his own voice to the show, Dierks has also gotten other popular performers to take part. Eric Church, Florida Georgia Line, and Thomas Rhett are just a few of the artists who have lent their time and talents to the event.

In 2015, Dierks told *Rolling Stone*, "We go over to the Vanderbilt Children's Hospital every year to present the check and meet some families, and I have some personal relationships with people there after 10 years. It's really good to go over there and see how lucky you are to have healthy kids, and if you didn't, this is where you'd want them to be. They have the best staff, the best

Now that Dierks is famous, he uses his celebrity status for good causes.

Dierks founded the Miles and Music for Kids motorcycle ride and concert to raise money for Nashville's Vanderbilt Children's Hospital.

Dierks enjoys performing for worthy causes. He is seen here in 2016 playing at "Nashville for Africa," a benefit for the African Children's Choir.

doctors, they make it feel like home even though it's a hospital."

Dierks also recently started performing a new job. In 2016, he co-hosted the Academy of Country Music Awards ceremony in Las Vegas, Nevada. He shared the stage with fellow musician Luke Bryan. At first, Dierks wasn't entirely comfortable with the idea of this new role. His anxiety actually pushed him to say yes to the opportunity.

Dierks says that he is always looking for new opportunities and challenges. He knew hosting was the right thing for him when he realized how uncomfortable it made him. When something makes Dierks feel nervous, he sees it as a sign that he is not pushing himself as much as he should. Having Luke alongside him for the adventure helped. He had no doubt that his fellow musician would keep things interesting.

Fans found Dierks and Luke to be fun and entertaining co-hosts. They were invited back to co-host in 2017. In addition to his hosting responsibilities,

Dierks and Luke Bryan joke around beside a life-size wax figure of Bryan at the ACM Awards in 2017.

Dierks was also nominated for three awards at the 2017 show—Male Vocalist of the Year, Album of the Year for *Black*, and Vocal Event of the Year for "Different for Girls." The musician who had taken home the trophy for Best New Artist 13 years earlier was clearly still going strong.

A Legend in the Making

Life has changed a lot for Dierks since his early days in Nashville. He started out as a single guy struggling to find a record deal. Now he is a happily married father of three with more than a dozen number-one hits. Sometimes it strikes him just how long he has been working as a successful musician. Shortly before his 2017 appearance at the Stagecoach Festival in Indio, California, he recalled the first time he performed at the popular event. It had been 2008 and he joked that it was so long ago that Taylor Swift had been *his* opening act. The tour was Swift's first, and Dierks remembers her as being incredibly poised. He knew then that she was going to accomplish great things in her career.

Life has changed a lot for Dierks since his early days in Nashville.

Many artists who have been around as long as Dierks have watched their popularity decline as time goes by. With so many talented performers out there, the music industry is fiercely competitive. Yet Dierks is more popular than ever. His eighth album, *Black*, gave the singer his biggest sales week of all time.

Dierks is seen here performing at the 2017 Stagecoach Festival in Indio, California.

The album sold 88,000 copies during the first seven days after its release in June, 2016.

After working so hard for his success, Dierks is both pleased and surprised by the fact that he is still at the top of the country music scene. He is grateful to be playing to his biggest audiences after touring for more than 13 years. He is also producing some of the biggest hits of his career. He has said that his success hasn't come the way he thought it would. He had hoped it would happen much sooner. But he also says that he wouldn't change a thing about it. Instead of taking it for granted, he just keeps putting more into it.

1975 Frederick Dierks Bentley is born on November 20.

1989 Dierks meets Cassidy Black, who will become his wife one day.

2004 He wins the Academy of Country Music award for Best New Artist.

2005 Dierks and Cassidy reunite and marry.

2008 He and Cassidy welcome their first child, a daughter named Evalyn.

2010 The couple's second daughter, Jordan, is born.

2013 A son, Knox, joins the family.

2016 Dierks releases his 15th number-one song, "Different for Girls," a duet with Elle King. He co-hosts the Academy of Country Music Awards with Luke Bryan for the first time.

2017 Dierks repeats as co-host of the ACM Awards with Luke Bryan.

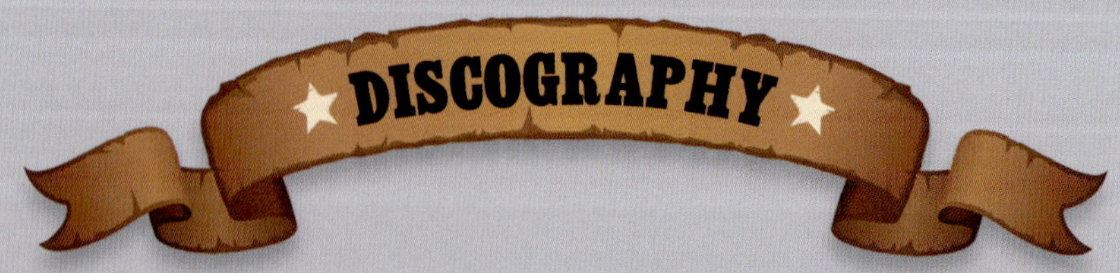

2003 *Dierks Bentley*
2005 *Modern Day Drifter*
2006 *Long Trip Alone*
2009 *Feel That Fire*
2010 *Up on the Ridge*
2012 *Home*
2014 *Riser*
2016 *Black*

Clay, Levi. *Country Guitar for Beginners*. Hove, United Kingdom: Fundamental Changes, 2016.

Paiva, Johannah Gilman. *Guess How Much I Love Nashville*. Oakville, Ontario: Flowerpot Children's Press, 2015.

VanVoorst, Jenny Fretland. *What's Great About Tennessee?* Minneapolis: Lerner, 2014.

On the Internet

Academy of Country Music
http://www.acmcountry.com/

Country Music Television
http://www.cmt.com/music

Dierks Bentley: The Official Website
http://www.dierks.com/

Works Consulted

———. "20 Questions With Dierks Bentley." CMT, June 4, 2004. http://www.cmt.com/news/1488164/20-questions-with-dierks-bentley/

———. "Dierks Bentley." Billboard. http://www.billboard.com/artist/300932/dierks-bentley/biography

———. "Dierks Bentley Leaves Big Country for Bluegrass." NPR, June 24, 2010. http://www.npr.org/templates/story/story.php?storyId=127563071

———. "Dierks Bentley Purchases Custom Cirrus Airplane." SoundsLikeNashville, October 9, 2012. http://www.soundslikenashville.com/news/dierks-bentley-purchases-custom-cirrus-plane/

———. "Dierks Bentley Welcomes Son Knox." *People*, October 10, 2013. http://celebritybabies.people.com/2013/10/10/dierks-bentley-welcomes-son-knox/

Asker, Jim. "In the 'Black': Dierks Bentley Bows at No. 1 on Top Country Albums with Best Sales Week Ever." *Billboard*, June 7, 2016. http://www.billboard.com/articles/columns/chart-beat/7400180/country-charts-dierks-bentley-thomas-rhett

Bonaguro, Alison. "Dierks Bentley: Performing for Fans is What He Loves." CMT, August 26, 2016. http://www.cmt.com/news/1770285/dierks-bentley-performing-for-fans-is-what-he-loves/

Casey, Jim. "Dierks Bentley and Elle King's 'Different for Girls' Wins CMA Award for Musical Event of the Year." Nash Country Daily, November 2, 2016. http://www.nashcountrydaily.com/2016/11/02/dierks-bentley-and-elle-kings-different-for-girls-wins-cma-award-for-musical-event-of-the-year/

Dauphin, Chuck. "Dierks Bentley & Elle King on Why 'Different for Girls' Is a Different Kind of Country Hit." *Billboard*, October 5, 2016. http://www.billboard.com/articles/columns/country/7533424/dierks-bentley-elle-king-different-for-girls-interview

Hudak, Joseph. "Dierks Bentley on New Album 'Black': I've Claimed the Right to Be Me." *Rolling Stone*, May 27, 2016. http://www.rollingstone.com/music/news/dierks-bentley-on-new-album-black-ive-claimed-the-right-to-be-me-20160527

Jason the 200-lb. Cowboy. "ACM Memories: Dierks Bentley." 99.5 WYCD, April 14, 2015. http://wycd.cbslocal.com/2015/04/14/acm-memories-dierks-bentley/

Kat, Nashville. "Dierks Bentley Opens Up About His Childhood and Finds a Fan in Bruce Springsteen." Taste of Country, March 22, 2011. http://tasteofcountry.com/dierks-bentley-childhood-bruce-springsteen/

Leon, Anya. "Dierks Bentley: I Became a Man When I Met My Wife (And Had Kids)." *People*, October 3, 2014. http://celebritybabies.people.com/2014/10/03/dierks-bentley-esquire-wife-pilots-license/

Lewis, Randy. "Stagecoach 2017: Dierks Bentley recalls when Taylor Swift opened for me." *Los Angeles Times*, April 29, 2017. http://www.latimes.com/entertainment/music/la-et-ms-stagecoach-dierks-bentley-backstage-20170429-story.html

Parton, Chris. "Dierks Bentley Marks Decade of Miles and Music With Big Stars, Huge Check." *Rolling Stone*, November 2, 2015. http://www.rollingstone.com/music/news/dierks-bentley-marks-decade-of-miles-and-music-with-big-stars-huge-check-20151102

Radloff, Jessica. "Dierks Bentley Reveals the Story Behind His Name and How He Knew His Wife Was the One." *Glamour*, May 26, 2015. http://www.glamour.com/story/dierks-bentley-reveals-the-sto

Remzy, Jeffrey B. "With pressure on, Dierks Bentley does it again." Country Standard Time, May 2005. http://www.countrystandardtime.com/d/article.asp?xid=279

Reuter, Annie. "Dierks Bentley & Elle King Tour Grand Ole Opry." Radio.com, October 27, 2016. http://radio.com/2016/10/27/dierks-bentley-elle-king-tour-grand-ole-opry/

Sculley, Alan. "Dierks Bentley is most comfortable on stage." *Wichita Eagle*, April 26, 2017. http://www.kansas.com/entertainment/music-news-reviews/article147014449.html

Stefano, Angela. "2017 ACM Awards Winners List." The Boot, April 2, 2017. http://theboot.com/2017-acm-awards-winners/

Thompson, Gayle. "41 Years Ago: Dierks Bentley Is Born in Phoenix." The Boot, November 20, 2016. http://theboot.com/dierks-bentley-birthday/

Thompson, Gayle. "Dierks Bentley is 'A Little Uneasy' About Hosting the 2016 ACM Awards." March 13, 2016. http://theboot.com/dierks-bentley-2016-acm-awards/

Thompson, Gayle. "Dierks Bentley is 'Grateful' to Share his Success with Wife Cassidy." The Boot, March 31, 2016. http://theboot.com/dierks-bentley-wife-cassidy-black/

Thompson, Gayle. "Dierks Bentley Reflects on Love of, Respect for Country Music at Hall of Fame Exhibit Opening." http://theboot.com/dierks-bentley-country-music-hall-of-fame-exhibit-details/

Todd, Roxanne. "Dierks Bentley riding high and hatless." Lancaster Online, September 24, 2004. http://lancasteronline.com/features/entertainment/dierks-bentley-riding-high-and-hatless/article_eca17502-fdf7-5ad6-b27b-47ca0424f10d.html

Waddell, Ray. "Dierks Bentley on His Success: 'I Don't Know How the Hell I'm Here." *Billboard*, August 20, 2014. http://www.billboard.com/articles/6221988/dierks-bentley-interview-headlining-tour-success

Whitten, Christine. "Dierks Bentley." *Arizona Foothills*, 2017. http://www.arizonafoothillsmagazine.com/features/features/1113-dierks-bentley.html

Whitfield, Bethany. "Famous Pilots Reminisce: Love at First Flight." October 3, 2014. http://www.flyingmag.com/pilots-places/pilots-adventures-more/famous-pilots-reminisce-love-first-flight

INDEX